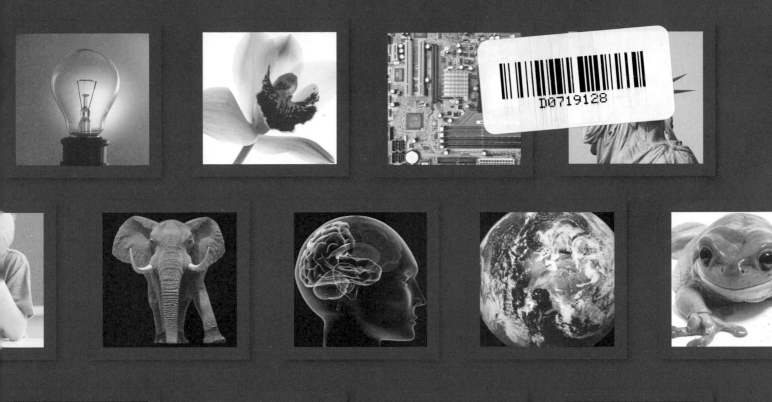

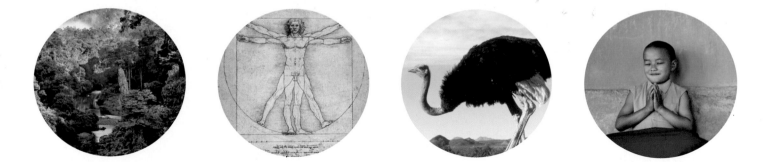

CHILDREN'S PHOTOGRAPHIC REFERENCE
ENCYCLOPEDIA
OF EVERYTHING

This edition published by Parragon Books Ltd in 2013

Parragon Books Ltd
Chartist House
15–17 Trim Street
Bath BA1 1HA, UK
www.parragon.com

ISBN 978-1-4723-2442-9

Printed in China

CHILDREN'S PHOTOGRAPHIC REFERENCE
ENCYCLOPEDIA OF EVERYTHING

PaRragon

Bath • New York • Singapore • Hong Kong • Cologne • Delhi
Melbourne • Amsterdam • Johannesburg • Shenzhen

CONTENTS

THE UNIVERSE AND PLANET EARTH

THE NATURAL WORLD

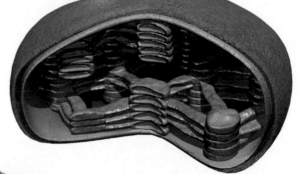

THE HUMAN BODY

HISTORY

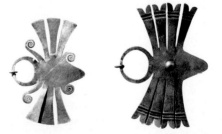

SCIENCE AND CULTURE

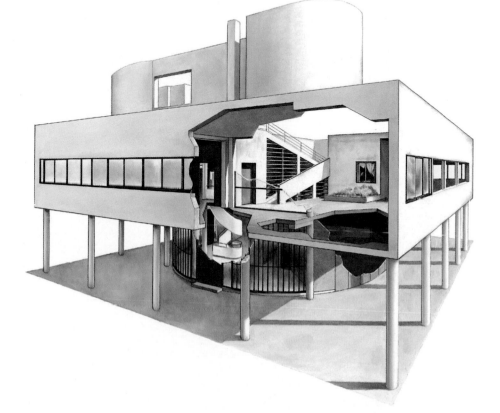

THE UNIVERSE AND PLANET EARTH

The Universe is an unimaginably huge place. It contains billions of galaxies, and each galaxy contains billions of stars. Around one of those stars, the Sun, orbits the planet Earth. Our planet is the only place in the Universe that we know contains life. Scientists are constantly discovering amazing new facts about the Universe. The one thing we know for sure is that there is still plenty that we have yet to find out.

EARTHRISE
The Earth appears over the horizon on the Moon. This picture was taken from the spaceship Apollo 10 while it was in orbit around the Moon.

Our Universe

The Universe is all the matter, energy, space and time that exists. It is constantly expanding in all directions. The Universe contains things that we can see, such as galaxies, stars, planets, nebulae and comets, and things that we cannot see, such as dark matter. Throughout history, scientists have made many discoveries about our Universe, but much about it is still mysterious and unknown.

STAR
Stars are made of shining gas, which gives off light and heat. The hottest stars are a blue-white colour, while the coolest are orange, yellow or red.

PLANET
The planets are sphere-shaped bodies that do not give off their own light. They orbit stars.

4,000
The number of stars that can be seen by the naked eye.

SATELLITE
Satellites do not have their own light. They orbit planets. One planet may have many satellites.

LIGHT YEAR
A light year is a unit of length equal to the distance travelled by light in one year. Light years are used to measure the huge distances between stars, planets, satellites and other bodies in the Universe.

1 LIGHT YEAR = 9,461,000,000,000 km

DARK MATTER

Most of the material in space is a strange substance that we cannot see. Scientists call it dark matter. There is much more dark matter than visible matter in the Universe, but we know very little about it.

NEBULA

A nebula is a cloud of gases and dust that can produce dazzling light displays. Sometimes, new stars form from these clouds. The nebulae themselves have formed from the material left over when a star dies.

LOOK AT THE SKY

All the stars we see when we look at the night sky are part of our galaxy, the Milky Way.

GALAXY

The galaxies are large groups of stars, planets, gases and dust that are held together by gravity. There are billions of galaxies in the Universe, and the largest have as many as 100 trillion stars.

In the future, they may even disappear.

1

THE START
At the beginning of time and space, the Universe was a tiny, hot, dense spot.

2

THE EXPLOSION
The Universe grew extremely quickly in the first fraction of a second after the Big Bang. Larger particles of matter formed and clumps of gas also appeared.

BEST THEORY

Today, most scientists accept that the Big Bang is the best way to explain how the Universe formed. The Ukrainian astronomer George Gamow was one of the first people to develop this theory in the 1940s. For many years, it was a very controversial idea.

THEORIES

Theories are explanations of natural events that are made after looking at the evidence. A theory can never be completely proved, but more evidence can be gathered to support the theory so that it becomes the best explanation we have.

3

GALAXIES

In the first 1 billion years after the Big Bang, the first galaxies formed. The galaxies are made up of dust, gas, planets and billions of stars.

4

THE SOLAR SYSTEM

About 9 billion years after the Big Bang, the Solar System, containing our Earth, appeared.

125
BILLION

An estimate of the number of galaxies in the visible Universe. There may be many more.

The life cycle of stars

Stars are huge spheres of burning gas. We see them as lights in the sky, but in fact, they vary greatly in size, colour and heat. Most appear white but some are orange, red or blue. Stars do not burn forever. Large stars have more fuel and they burn it quickly. They last about 10 million years. Small stars may last for hundreds of billions of years.

BIG STARS

With a mass eight or more times greater than our Sun, these massive stars have a short life. When they come to the end of their lives, their centres collapse. This causes a huge explosion called a supernova, which can shine as brightly as a whole galaxy.

2 COLOUR
Massive stars are blue-white in colour.

3 RED GIANT
Near the end of their lives, all stars become red giants. They become bigger and their temperature drops.

1 STAR BIRTH
The force of gravity pulls the dust and gas together in clouds called nebulae. The material condenses, its temperature rises and it begins to shine. A star has been born.

2 COLOUR
Less massive stars are a pale red colour because their temperature is lower. Small stars, called red dwarfs, are the most common type of star in the Universe.

SMALL STARS

These less massive stars have a much longer life than the most massive stars, eventually turning into red giants after many billions of years.

4 SUPERNOVA
A supernova is a massive explosion that is caused when a star collapses at the end of its life.

5 NEUTRON STAR
A supernova may leave behind a small, dense body called a neutron star.

4.5
BILLION YEARS
The age of the Sun.

3 RED GIANT
Like all stars, less massive stars become red giants. Their size increases and their temperature drops.

4 NEBULA
At the end of its life, the gases near the surface of the star start to drift off to form a cloud called a planetary nebula.

5 WHITE DWARF
After the star has shed its outer layers of gas, it leaves a white dwarf. This shines a bright white colour before it eventually goes out.

The galaxies are groups of moving stars, planets, gas and dust that are held together by the force of gravity. The first galaxies formed 200 million years after the Big Bang.

ONE GALAXY?

Until the start of the 20th century, it was believed that the Milky Way was the only galaxy.

STARS
Galaxies contain billions of stars. Most of them are grouped near the centre.

GRAVITY
Every object in the Universe pulls every other object towards it with a force called gravity. The force is greater the larger the objects are and the closer together they are. Galaxies are held together by gravity.

MILKY WAY
The galaxy that contains the Earth is called the Milky Way. It is a spiral galaxy. We are situated in one of the spiral arms. The stars we see in the night sky are just a few of the billions of stars in the Milky Way.

KINDS OF GALAXY

ELLIPTICAL
These are sphere-shaped galaxies that are made up mostly of old stars. They contain very little dust or gas.

SPIRAL
Spiral galaxies are made up of old and new stars, which form a spiral shape like a slowly turning pinwheel.

IRREGULAR
Galaxies with no regular shape are called irregular. These galaxies contain a lot of new stars.

DUST AND G...
Galaxies are ... dust and gases.

COLLIDING GALAXIES
Sometimes two spiral galaxies collide with each other. In time, these galaxies will join to form

MORE THAN
100 BILLION
The number of stars in the Milky Way.

The Solar System

The Sun is the closest star to our planet. Eight planets orbit the Sun. Many smaller objects also orbit the Sun, including dwarf planets, asteroids and comets. The Sun and all the other bodies that orbit it, are together known as the Solar System.

RINGS
Saturn's rings are formed from small particles that are orbiting the planet.

GAS GIANTS
The outer planets – Jupiter, Saturn, Uranus and Neptune – are enormous spheres made of mostly gas. These planets are known as gas giants and are very cold at their surfaces.

NEPTUNE

URANUS

SATURN

YEARS
The time it takes for a planet to complete one orbit of the Sun is the length of the planet's year. The further away a planet is from the Sun, the longer its year.

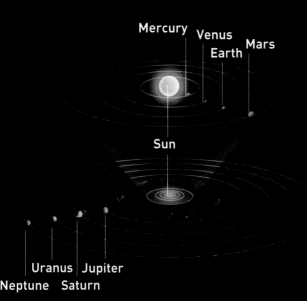

Mercury
Venus
Earth
Mars

Sun

Uranus Jupiter
Neptune Saturn

MOONS
The outer planets are orbited by many moons. Saturn and Jupiter have more than 60 moons each.

150
million km
The distance from the Sun to Earth.

ASTEROID BELT
This region of the
Solar System
contains millions
of pieces of rock.

DAYS
Each planet rotates
around its own axis.
The time it takes to
do one rotation is
the length of the
planet's day.

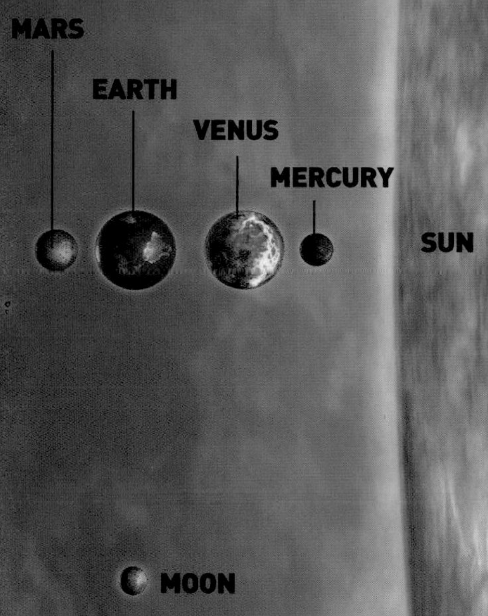

MARS

EARTH

VENUS

MERCURY

SUN

JUPITER

MOON

ROCKY PLANETS
Orbiting between the
Sun and the asteroid belt are
four smaller rocky planets.
All except Mercury are
surrounded by atmospheres.
Mercury and Venus are very
hot, while the surface of
Mars is colder than Earth.

BIGGEST PLANET
Jupiter is the biggest
of the eight planets.
Its volume is more
than 1,000 times
greater than the Earth.

The Sun

The Sun is the only star in the Solar System. It is a medium-sized star that formed 4.5 billion years ago. It has about 5 billion years of life left. Its light and heat make life possible on our planet.

8.5 MINS

The time it takes for light to travel from the surface of the Sun to the Earth.

SHINING GASES

The Sun is made mostly of hydrogen (90 per cent) and helium (10 per cent). These two gases are very hot, making the Sun shine.

CORE
The Sun's core is 15 million °C.

FACT FILE

Symbol	
Distance from the Earth	149.9 million km
Diameter	1,391,000 km
Temperature at surface	6,000 °C

RADIATION ZONE
Energy from the core passes through this zone.

CONVECTION ZONE
Energy is carried to the surface of the Sun in the convection zone.

PHOTOSPHERE
The part of the Sun that we can see, made up of the surface and the atmosphere, is the photosphere. The temperature here is 6000 °C.

ECLIPSE

When the Moon passes between the Sun and the Earth, this causes a solar eclipse. It goes dark on Earth for a few minutes.

SOLAR WIND

A continuous 'wind' of particles is given off in all directions by the Sun. Near the Earth, the solar wind has a speed of 450 kilometres per second. It causes weather events such as the northern lights and magnetic storms.

CORONA

The outer part of the atmosphere stretches many millions of kilometres into space. It is 2 million °C.

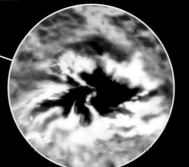

SUNSPOTS

Sunspots are darker areas on the Sun's surface where the gases are cooler.

FLARES

Flares are extremely powerful explosions on the surface of the Sun that throw up huge amounts of material into space.

The Earth

Sun

Earth

O ur planet is the third closest to the Sun and the largest of the rocky planets. It is known as the Blue Planet because of the colour of the oceans that cover two-thirds of the surface. The Earth is the only planet where liquid water has been found on its surface.

WATER
Clouds form from water vapour in the air that has condensed back into liquid.

ATMOSPHERE
The atmosphere is made up of several gases, mainly nitrogen and oxygen.

LIFE

The Earth is the only planet where life is known to exist. There are several reasons why life can exist on our planet: the presence of liquid water at the surface, temperatures that are neither too hot nor too cold, and a protective atmosphere. The Earth is also the only planet where there is water in all three states:

SOLID
Water freezes at 0 °C. At the poles, the coldest places on the planet, water is frozen.

LIQUID
A large part of the Earth's surface is covered in liquid water. Most of it is salt water.

GAS
Water exists in the air as water vapour. It condenses back into liquid to form clouds.

HUMAN ACTIVITY
Humans put harmful chemicals into the atmosphere when they burn coal, oil and gas.

SOUTH POLE

NORTH POLE

AXIS OF ROTATION
The axis around
which the
Earth spins.

STRUCTURE

The Earth is made up of different layers.
The outermost layer is the atmosphere,
which is made up of a mixture of gases.
Under this is the surface, which is mostly
covered in water. The surface is the top of
a thin, solid crust. Under the crust is the
mantle. At the centre is the solid core.

Mantle

Core

Atmosphere

Crust

FACT FILE

Symbol	⊕
Distance from the Sun	149.9 million km
Diameter	12,756 km
Average temperature	15 °C
Moons	1

3

The percentage of
water on the surface
of the Earth that is
fresh water.

GRAVITY

We are held onto the surface of the
Earth by the force of gravity. Gravity
gives us our weight. The strength of a
planet's gravitational pull depends on
its size, and we would weigh different
amounts on other planets or on the
Moon. For example, the same person
would weigh these amounts:

70 kg
on Earth

11 kg
on Moon

177 kg
on Jupiter

The Earth's movements

23.5°
The angle at which Earth is tilted.

Like all the planets in the Solar System, the Earth spins on its own axis and it also orbits the Sun. These two movements cause the difference between day and night and the changing of the seasons.

21 JUNE
The longest day in the northern hemisphere happens on the summer solstice.

YEARLY ORBIT

The Earth takes 365 days, 5 hours and 48 minutes to orbit the Sun. As the Earth spins on its tilted axis, the regions change throughout the year depending on their distance from the Sun. This is what causes the change of the seasons as well as the length of our days and nights.

SUN

21 SEPTEMBER
This is the autumn equinox in the northern hemisphere. Day and night are the same length – both 12 hours.

147.5 MILLION KM

— AXIS OF ROTATION

DAILY ROTATION

The Earth turns around its own axis each day. This movement causes day and night. It also makes the planet slightly flattened at the poles, and causes ocean currents.

PLEASE NOTE: FOR THE PURPOSES OF THIS DIAGRAM THE EARTH AND THE SUN ARE NOT SHOWN TO SCALE.

21 DECEMBER
This is the winter solstice in the northern hemisphere. It is the shortest day of the year.

152.5 MILLION KM

21 MARCH
This is the spring equinox in the northern hemisphere. Day and night are the same length.

LEAP YEAR
Every fourth year, the month of February has 29 days instead of 28. This is called a leap year.

NORTHERN HEMISPHERE

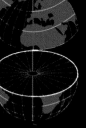

EQUATOR

SOUTHERN HEMISPHERE

HEMISPHERES
The Earth is divided into two halves: the northern and southern hemispheres. The equator is the imaginary line that separates the two hemispheres. When it is summer in the north, it is winter in the south.

JET LAG
Long-distance flights can cause jet lag. This is because a change in time zones can upset our body's natural rhythm.

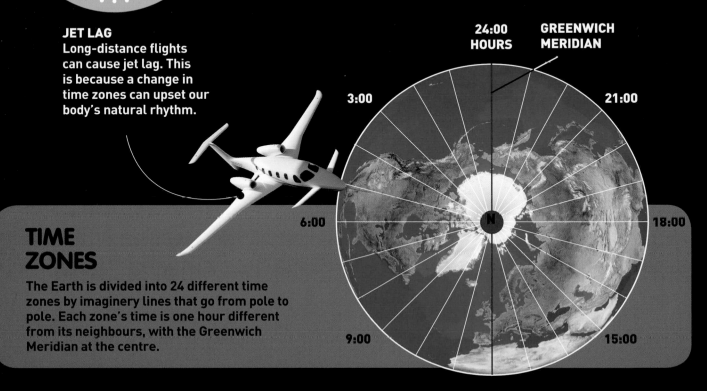

24:00 HOURS

GREENWICH MERIDIAN

3:00

21:00

6:00

18:00

9:00

15:00

12:00 HOURS

TIME ZONES
The Earth is divided into 24 different time zones by imaginery lines that go from pole to pole. Each zone's time is one hour different from its neighbours, with the Greenwich Meridian at the centre.

The Moon

The Moon is our planet's only natural satellite. It orbits the Earth with the same side always facing towards it. Seen from the Earth, the Moon changes shape depending on the light from the Sun that it reflects towards us.

FULL MOON

In myths and stories, a full moon, with its bright moonlit nights, was thought to cause strange happenings.

ORBIT

For each complete orbit, the Moon makes exactly one rotation. Because of this, the same side of the Moon always faces us.

MOON

MOON'S ORBIT

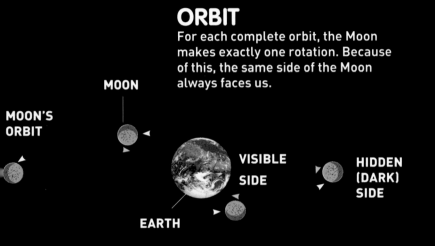

VISIBLE SIDE

HIDDEN (DARK) SIDE

EARTH

CRATERS

The Moon's surface is covered in craters caused by the impact of asteroids and comets.

THE TIDES

The Moon's gravity pulls at the water in the Earth's oceans. This causes the tides. At the point where the Moon is directly overhead, its pull on the Earth's water is strongest, and the water rises to cause a high tide. There is also a high tide at the opposite side to this, where the Moon's pull is least strong. High tides happen about once every 12 hours.

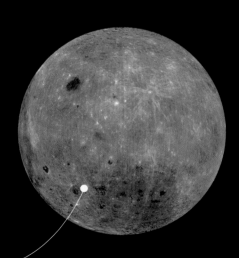

SEAS

These areas appear dark to us. Despite their name, they are dry.

DARK SIDE

The dark side of the Moon cannot be seen from the Earth. It was first photographed by a Russian space probe in 1959.

29.5 DAYS

The average length of the Moon's orbit.

CORE
The Moon probably has a solid core, but we do not know for sure.

MANTLE
This rocky part is about 1,000 km thick.

FACT FILE

Symbol	☽
Distance from the Earth	384,400 km
Diameter	3,476 km
Temperature	100 ºC (day) -100 ºC (night)

PHASES OF THE MOON
The amount of the Moon that we can see changes during the Moon's orbit. We see a full moon when the Earth is between the Moon and the Sun. When the Moon is between the Earth and the Sun, the Moon is entirely in shade. This is a new moon.

New Moon	Waxing Crescent	First Quarter	Waxing Gibbous	Full Moon	Waning Gibbous	Third Quarter	Waning Crescent

The early Earth

The Earth and the other planets in the Solar System first formed 4.6 billion years ago. At first, the Earth was a huge ball of burning rock, with no water or atmosphere. Over the course of millions of years, great changes took place. First the Earth's crust formed, then the atmosphere, the oceans, and finally the continents, as the Earth became the planet that we know today.

1

FORMATION
The Earth formed from a huge cloud of gas and dust.

2

COOLING
Little by little, the surface cooled to form a dry crust.

10

MOUNTAIN RANGES
The highest mountain ranges, such as the Alps, the Andes and the Himalayas, started to form about 60 million years ago.

9

THE FIRST CONTINENTS
Land started to appear 1.8 billion years ago. Little by little, it grew into a huge mass of land, which later broke up into the continents we know today.

4 BILLION YEARS

The age of the oldest rocks.

LIFE
When the atmosphere formed and liquid water appeared, the first life started to evolve.

ASTEROID AND COMET IMPACT
Without an atmosphere to protect it, the surface of the Earth was struck by the impact of asteroids and comets.

SUPERVOLCANOES
Burning material exploded through the crust in the form of huge volcanoes.

THE ATMOSPHERE
The gases given off by the volcanoes formed a layer around the planet.

THE FIRST RAIN
Volcanoes created water vapour, which condensed in the atmosphere to form clouds.

THE FIRST ICE AGE
About 2.4 billion years ago, the planet cooled enough for the surface to freeze.

THE SEAS AND OCEANS
As the crust cooled, liquid water built up on the surface to create oceans and seas.

Structure of the Earth

The Earth is very different under its surface. The rocky ground on which we live is only a thin crust. Underneath the crust is the mantle, made of solid and liquid rock, and in the centre is a hot metal core. The whole planet is surrounded by a layer of gases that form the atmosphere.

HOW FAR HAVE WE EXPLORED?

From the surface to the centre of the Earth it is more than 6000 km. So far, we have managed to explore 12 kilometres down.

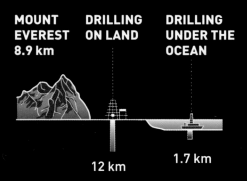

MOUNT EVEREST 8.9 km

DRILLING ON LAND

DRILLING UNDER THE OCEAN

12 km

1.7 km

ATMOSPHERE 1,000 km

THE EARTH 6,378 km

700

km

2,270 km

1,216 km

INNER CORE
The inner core is made of solid iron and nickle.

OUTER CORE
The outer core is made of molten iron and nickel.

OUTER MANTLE
The movement of the outer mantle causes earthquakes and volcanoes.

INNER MANTLE
Heavy rocks make up the mantle. They are at more than 1000 °C.

SOLAR
RADIATION

SOLAR
RADIATION

NO ATMOSPHERE
Life would be
wiped out by the
radiation and heat.

ATMOSPHERE
Filters the Sun's rays
and distributes its heat

MESOSPHERE

STRATOSPHERE

THE ATMOSPHERE
The atmosphere is made up of a mixture
of gases, mainly nitrogen and oxygen.
It is divided into different layers
depending on the amount of gases at
each height. The atmosphere gives us
the air we breathe and it protects us
from the Sun's harmful rays.

CRUST
This outer layer of
rock is 6–70 km thick.

**HOT
PLANET**
The temperature of
the Earth rises the
closer you get to
the centre.

THE HYDROSPHERE
The hydrosphere is the name for the liquid part of the Earth, including
the oceans, lakes, rivers, groundwater and water in the atmosphere.
Water covers more than two-thirds of the Earth's surface.

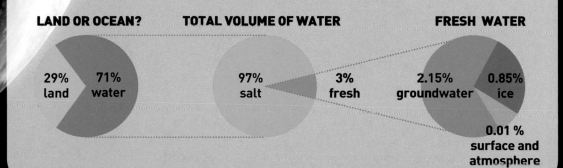

LAND OR OCEAN?	TOTAL VOLUME OF WATER	FRESH WATER
29% land 71% water	97% salt 3% fresh	2.15% groundwater 0.85% ice
		0.01 % surface and atmosphere

The continents

The Earth's crust is made up of parts that fit together like the pieces in a jigsaw puzzle. Called tectonic plates, they float on top of the semi-liquid mantle and are continually moving. The movements of the plates caused different continents to form millions of years ago, and even today, the continents are still on the move.

250 MILLION YEARS AGO
The Tethys Ocean slowly divided Pangea into two subcontinents: Laurasia and Gondwana. They joined together again to make a super-continent.

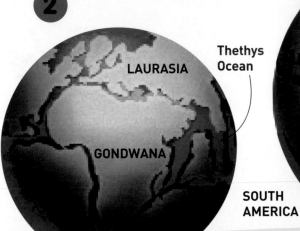

LAURASIA

Thethys Ocean

GONDWANA

SOUTH AMERICA

290 MILLION YEARS AGO
There was one block of land, called Pangea, surrounded by water.

PANGEA

1-10 CM
The distance the tectonic plates move each year.

CONTINENTAL DRIFT
We live on plates that are continually, but slowly, moving the continents around the Earth. This process is called continental drift.

GREAT FORCES
Hot molten rock (magma) rises from the centre of the Earth, while cooler magma sinks. This movement causes the huge forces that move the tectonic plates.

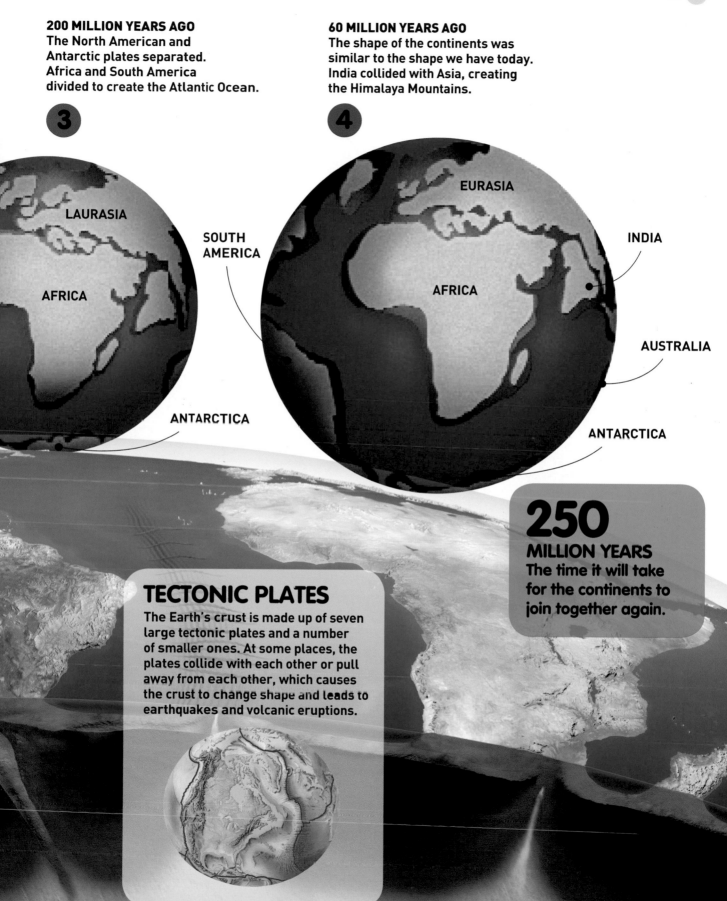

200 MILLION YEARS AGO
The North American and Antarctic plates separated. Africa and South America divided to create the Atlantic Ocean.

3

LAURASIA

AFRICA

SOUTH AMERICA

ANTARCTICA

60 MILLION YEARS AGO
The shape of the continents was similar to the shape we have today. India collided with Asia, creating the Himalaya Mountains.

4

EURASIA

INDIA

AFRICA

AUSTRALIA

ANTARCTICA

TECTONIC PLATES

The Earth's crust is made up of seven large tectonic plates and a number of smaller ones. At some places, the plates collide with each other or pull away from each other, which causes the crust to change shape and leads to earthquakes and volcanic eruptions.

250
MILLION YEARS
The time it will take for the continents to join together again.

THE NATURAL WORLD

Living organisms come in lots of different shapes and sizes. They range from tiny bacteria that are too small to see, to giant trees that are more than 100 metres tall. Millions of different types, or species, have developed over billions of years in a process called evolution.

INSECT HUNTER
Chameleons have long sticky tongues, which they use to catch insects. They are a type of animal called a reptile (see page 54–55).

The plant kingdom

There are about 350,000 different plant species. Plants make their own food using sunlight and a special green substance called chlorophyll. This process is called photosynthesis. Most plants are attached to the ground.

1 GREEN ALGAE

Some algae live on land, in moist conditions on trees, among plants or even in piles of rubbish. They use photosynthesis to make their own food, but they do not have leaves and roots. Today, only green algae (left) are included in the plant kingdom. Other types of algae have their own separate kingdom.

9,550

The age in years of the oldest Norwegian spruce (a kind of pine tree), found in Sweden.

2 BRYOPHYTES

Bryophytes do not have tissues to transport water and nutrients around the plant. These plants include mosses (below).

3 SEEDLESS

Seedless plants reproduce using tiny spores. The spores do not have a store of food. Ferns (left) are the best-known plants in this group.

CLASSIFICATION

Almost all plants are flowering plants. They are called angiosperms. Many plants are vascular. This means that they have special tissues inside them to transport nutrients around the plant.

Plant kingdom
- Green algae

- Non-vascular plants
  - Bryophytes

- Vascular plants
  - Seedless plants
  - Seed plants
    - Angiosperms (flowering plants)
    - Gymnosperms

SENSITIVE
Saffron flowers open or close depending on the temperature.

4 ANGIOSPERMS

These plants make seeds, flowers and fruit. Angiosperms are found on every continent except Antarctica. They reproduce using flowers, which develop into fruits with seeds inside them. They come in many shapes and sizes and include roses, orchids (above), wheat, coffee plants and oak trees.

FUNGI

Fungi, such as mushrooms and moulds, are not plants, but have their own separate kingdom. They do not have chlorophyll to make their food. They feed on animals and other plants that are either dead or alive.

5 GYMNOSPERMS

These are plants that make seeds but not flowers. Conifers are examples of gymnosperms. They include pine trees (below) and trees such as cypress, larch and monkey puzzle.

Land plants

The earliest plants lived in water. Over millions of years, some of these plants gradually changed and were able to invade the land, living in damp places. Changes to their structure stopped them from losing water, and they could use the Sun's energy more effectively than water plants. Land plants first appeared on Earth almost 450 million years ago.

FERNS
The largest ferns grow up to 25 metres tall. Ferns live in damp, shady places.

FUNGI
Fungi live alongside land plants, feeding on them or combining with algae to form lichens.

TALLEST
Giant redwood trees are the tallest plants in the world. They can grow to more than 110 metres high.

EPIPHYTES
These plants grow
on other plants,
without fixing
themselves to
the ground.

TREES
The woody trunks
of trees give them
strength and allow
them to grow more
than 100 metres tall.

FLOWERS
Flowering plants
use their colourful
displays to attract
birds and insects.

CONQUERING THE LAND

Roots allow plants to grow on the land. They
fix the plant to the ground and take in water
and minerals from the soil.

The plant cuticle is a waterproof covering
that protects land plants from damage by the
wind or the Sun. Tiny holes called stomata
open and close to control water loss.

MOSSES
These are some
of the simplest of
all land plants.

60
The number of
centimetres a day some
species of bamboo can
grow. They are the
fastest-growing plants.

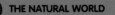

Ocean life

The oceans are the largest habitat on the Earth. Many different species live in the oceans. The sizes and shapes of the species change depending on the conditions and the food that is found in each ocean zone.

UP TO 500 METRES
In this zone, there is enough light for animals to see during the day.

TEMPERATURE
Water temperature is very important in deciding which species are found in each zone. There are five major climate zones in the planet's oceans (right).

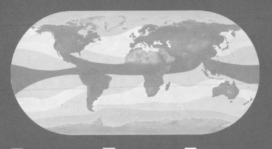

UP TO 4,000 METRES
There is no longer enough light for plant life and there is not a lot of food.

EQUATORIAL   TROPICAL   SUBTROPICAL
TEMPERATE   POLAR

ENDEMIC SPECIES
These are species that only live in one specific place. For example, the globefish on the left is found only in the tropical waters of the Atlantic Ocean.

MORE THAN 6,000 METRES
At this depth, it is extremely cold.

SURFACE LAYER
This zone is the warmest and has the most food. There is enough light for plants to grow.

MAKING YOUR OWN LIGHT
Some animals give off a greenish light. They use the light to attract prey or to surprise possible enemies.

UP TO 6,000 METRES
There is no light, the water is very cold and there is almost no food.

OCEANIC ZONES
Life in the oceans can be grouped into different layers according to how deep the water is. The deeper you go, the harder it becomes for creatures to live. There is less light and it becomes colder.

80
The number of marine species that are in danger of extinction.

Birds

Birds have bodies that are covered in feathers, and beaks with no teeth. Their wings are arms that have adapted for flight, although some birds can no longer fly. Birds are warm-blooded animals. They reproduce by laying eggs.

READY TO FLY

The shape of a bird's body and its feathers, allow it to stay in the air and to fly. Birds have strong muscles and light bones that are hollow and filled with air.

VARIETY

Birds are found in many different habitats, including water, air and land. Some birds are very small, such as the hummingbird, while others are very large, such as the ostrich, which is the largest bird of all.

PENGUIN
Can survive at temperatures of -60 °C in Antarctica.

WINGS
When they fly, birds use their wings to stay in the air, move forwards and change direction. The wings have special feathers to make this possible.

HUMMINGBIRD
Weight:
1.6 grams

OSTRICH
Weight:
125 kilograms

43 °C
The body temperature of birds.

BALANCE
Birds keep their balance when flying by using both their wings and their legs.

TAIL
Made of feathers, the tail helps the bird to keep its balance when it lands, and is used for steering and braking during flight.

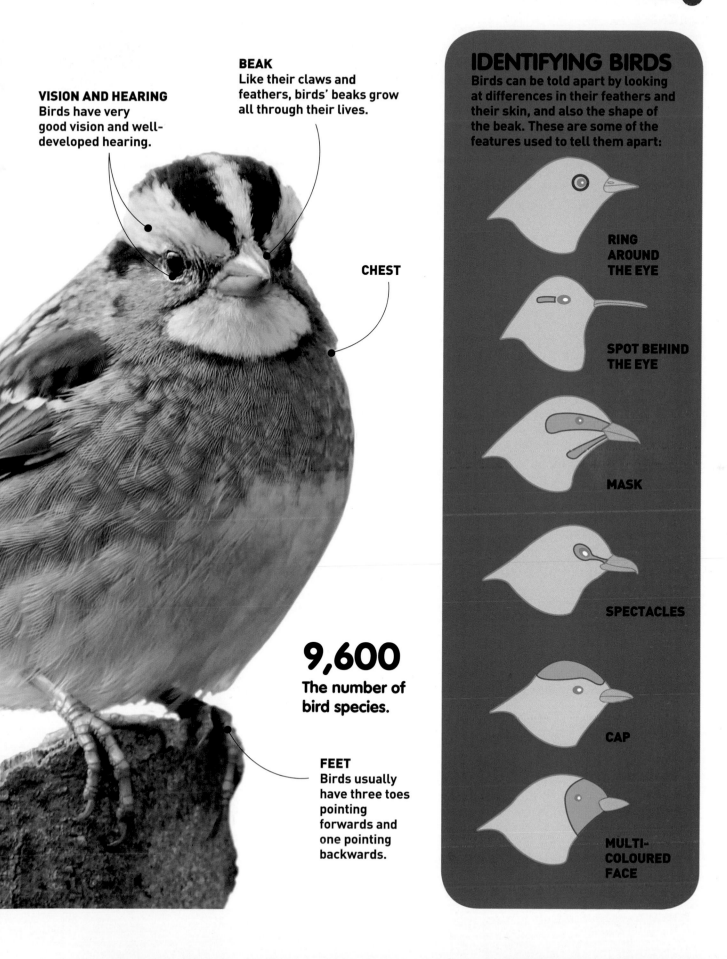

VISION AND HEARING
Birds have very good vision and well-developed hearing.

BEAK
Like their claws and feathers, birds' beaks grow all through their lives.

CHEST

9,600
The number of bird species.

FEET
Birds usually have three toes pointing forwards and one pointing backwards.

IDENTIFYING BIRDS
Birds can be told apart by looking at differences in their feathers and their skin, and also the shape of the beak. These are some of the features used to tell them apart:

RING AROUND THE EYE

SPOT BEHIND THE EYE

MASK

SPECTACLES

CAP

MULTI-COLOURED FACE

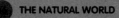

How birds fly

Most birds fly just by beating their wings, but some change between beating their wings and gliding. Beating wings uses a lot of energy, so birds have adapted the way they fly to suit their size and their needs. Larger birds have more powerful, but slower, wingbeats.

FLIGHT
For most birds, flying is not only a way to get around, but also of escaping predators, catching prey and showing off to a mate.

GLIDING
When it glides, a bird saves energy because it uses the wind to fly without beating its wings. The bird climbs with the help of air currents, gains height, then glides downwards until it reaches another current that will carry it back up again.

TAKE-OFF
The bird is already flying after a couple of beats of its wings.

GAINING HEIGHT
The angle of the wings and the wind allow the bird to climb.

GLIDING
It slowly goes lower in a glide.

FLYING IN A WAVE
In this way of flying, the bird beats its wings to gain height, then folds its wings and allows itself to fall. It then beats its wings again, using the strength gained by falling to go up again.

CLIMB
Bird beats its wings.

FALL
It keeps its wings folded next to its body.

GROUP FLYING

Flying together is a way of saving energy. The bird at the front of the group makes a pathway through the air, making it easier for the rest of the birds to fly. Normally, birds fly either in an 'L' shape – such as pelicans – or a 'V' shape – such as geese.

1

2

CHANGING PLACES
When the leader of the group tires, another bird takes its place.

LOWERING ITS WINGS
When it lowers its wings, the feathers close up again.

BEATING ITS WINGS

A bird flies through the air as if it were rowing with its wings. With each beat, the wings both keep the bird in the air and push it forwards.

GAINING MOMENTUM
With the wings behind the body, it gains the strength to raise its wings.

RAISING THE WINGS
From bottom to top, the feathers at the end of the wings separate.

50 km/h
The average speed of a pelican in flight when there is no wind.

FASTEST WINGBEAT

Hummingbirds fly only by beating their wings. They do not glide. A hummingbird can hover in the same place by beating its wings very quickly. Some species beat their wings up to 70 times a second. Hummingbirds are the only birds that can fly backwards.

1

2

3

Flightless birds

There are some species of bird that cannot fly. Some species are too heavy to take off. Others have lost their wings, or their wings have become very small. Some still have large wings but they no longer use them to fly. Flightless birds can be divided into those that live on land (terrestrial) and those that can swim (aquatic).

AQUATIC
Penguins are aquatic flightless birds. Their wings are shaped like flippers, which they use to swim quickly and skilfully.

WINGS
The wings have solid bones that allow the birds to remain underwater easily.

72 km/h
The top speed of an ostrich when it runs.

SWIMMERS
The penguin's feet have four webbed toes that point backwards. It uses its toes, wings and tail to swim and change direction.

DIVING
The wings work as flippers. It uses its feet and tail as a rudder.

BREATHING
Between dives, a penguin has to leap out of the water to breathe.

RESTING
When it rests, it swims very slowly using both its wings and legs.

BAD FLIERS

About 260 species of bird, including chickens, can only fly in short bursts. Instead, they use their legs to walk, run and scratch the earth.

1 Runs and jumps.

2 Awkward, fast flap of the wings.

3 Crash landing.

RUNNING

With their strong legs, many land birds can run at high speeds to escape a predator or to hunt prey.

TOE BONES

RUNNERS

The ratites are a group of land birds that are powerful runners. Their wings are very small and of no use for flying. Instead, they have developed strong legs, which they use to move around.

OSTRICH
This large bird uses its wings for balance when running.

KIWI
The kiwi has tiny wings, which are hard to see under its feathers.

CASSOWARY
This is a large bird with strong, well developed legs.

RHEA
With long legs and good vision, the rhea is a skilful hunter.

Life cycle of mammals

All animals go through the same basic stages in their life cycles: they are born, grow, reproduce and die. Among mammals, there are differences in how the animal reproduces, the length of pregnancy, how long the mother feeds its young and how long the animal lives. However, their life cycles all share the same stages.

READY TO REPRODUCE
A rabbit is ready to reproduce at 5–7 months, and a camel at 3–5 years.

LIVE YOUNG
The vital organs of the young develop inside the body of the mother.

90 YEARS
How long some species of whale live.

PRODUCING MILK
The infants of all mammals feed only on their mother's milk until they are old enough to digest solid food.

NUMBER OF YOUNG
In general, the larger the animal, the fewer young it gives birth to at the same time.

Cow
1

Goat
2–3
kids

Dog
3–8
puppies

Rat
6–12
babies

YOUNG
Rabbits give birth to 3–9 babies in each litter, and can have more than five litters in a year.

LENGTH OF PREGNANCY

ANIMAL	MONTHS
Elephant	22
Giraffe	15
Chimpanzee	9
Lion	4
Dog	2

MOVING AROUND
While it is still small, a baby koala clings to its mother's shoulders as she moves from place to place.

IN THE POUCH
When it is born, the infant stays in the pouch, where it feeds on its mother's milk.

PREGNANCY
Pregnancy is the period of time spent in the mother's womb. In rabbits, pregnancy lasts 28–33 days, while in elephants it lasts 22 months.

MARSUPIALS
Marsupials are pregnant for just 9–35 days, depending on the species. After they are born, the babies develop in their mother's pouch, which is a fold of skin at the front of the mother's body.

HUMANS
Humans belong to the group of mammals that give birth to live young.

MONOTREMES
Mammals that lay eggs are called monotremes. An echidna egg takes 12 days to hatch. After it has hatched, the baby echidna spends the next 50 days in its mother's pouch.

Mammals in danger

Scientists think that within the next 30 years, nearly a quarter of the species of mammals alive today may disappear altogether, becoming extinct.

15

The percentage of European mammal species that are in danger of extinction.

GIANT PANDA
Found in the south of China, the giant panda is in danger of extinction. The animal's natural habitat has been destroyed, and it is also hunted illegally.

LEVELS OF DANGER

Species in danger are labelled as vulnerable, endangered or critically endangered. These are the latest figures for mammals in danger (2012).

CRITICALLY ENDANGERED
188 species

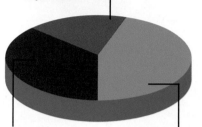

ENDANGERED
448 species

VULNERABLE
505 species

ORANGUTAN

The orangutan is found only on the islands of Borneo and Sumatra. The destruction of tropical rainforest and illegal buying and selling of the orangutans are the main threats to the species.

HUMAN CAUSES

The causes of extinction are habitat destruction and hunting.

IBERIAN LYNX

This wild cat is native to Spain and Portugal on the Iberian Peninsula. It is critically endangered. One reason for this is that there are fewer numbers of its main prey, the rabbit.

RHINOCEROS

Several species of rhinoceros are in danger of extinction because of illegal poaching.

THE HUMAN BODY

Our bodies are among the most complex structures in the Universe. Our brains alone contain more connections than all the computers on Earth put together! The human body is made up of many different organs, which all work together to keep us healthy.

MUSCLES

Just under our skin, a system of muscles enables us to move our bodies. Our facial muscles allow us to show our emotions in our expressions (see pages 86–87).

The cell

The human body is made up of billions of cells. The cells are so small that they can be seen only through a microscope. Each human cell is made up of the same parts: a nucleus and cytoplasm, surrounded by a membrane.

USEFUL LIFE
Some cells live for only 3–5 days. Others are active throughout a person's life.

CANCER
Sometimes cells go wrong and start growing uncontrollably. This can cause a disease called cancer. To cure cancer, the cells that have gone wrong need to be killed.

CYTOSKELETON
This is made up of strands that keep the cell's shape and allow it to move.

LYSOSOME
Lysosomes break down the cell's waste.

GOLGI APPARATUS
This processes and sends out the proteins made by the rough endoplasmic reticulum.

ROUGH ENDOPLASMIC RETICULUM
Makes and transports proteins.

100 BILLION
The number of cells in an adult human being's body. There are 210 different kinds of human cell.

CELL MEMBRANE
Covers and
protects the cell.

NUCLEUS
Controls
the activity,
growth and
reproduction
of the cell.

MITOSIS

Two new cells are made from one
cell in the process of mitosis. The
new cells are exactly the same as the
first cell. Mitosis allows an organism
to develop, grow and repair itself.
Some cells can divide about 50 times.

NUCLEOLUS
Made of ribonucleic
acid and protein.

DNA
This contains the
information that tells
the cell how to behave.

CYTOPLASM
The region between the cell
membrane and the nucleus.

**SMOOTH ENDOPLASMIC
RETICULUM**
Makes many different
substances that the
cell needs.

MITOCHONDRIA

Located in the cytoplasm, the mitochondria
are the parts of a cell that give it its energy.
There are many mitochondria in every cell,
with more in those cells that need greater
amounts of energy to do their work.

Circulatory system

The cells in our bodies need food and oxygen to live. They also need to have waste taken away from them. The system that does these jobs is called the circulatory system. Substances are carried to or from cells in the blood. Pumped by the heart, the blood reaches all parts of the body along a network of tubes called blood vessels.

BLOOD CIRCUIT

Blood travels around the circulatory system in a figure–of–eight shape, crossing at the heart. The main circuit carries red, oxygenated blood along the arteries from the heart to all parts of the body. The blood reaches individual cells through tiny blood vessels called capillaries. Blue deoxygenated blood returns to the heart along the veins.

SUBCLAVIAN VEIN
Connects the armpit to the superior vena cava.

JUGULAR VEINS
Four of these, two on each side of the neck.

BRACHIAL ARTERY
One in each arm.

LEFT CAROTID ARTERY

OTHER JOBS
The circulatory system also protects the body against infections and keeps its temperature at 37 °C.

SUPERIOR VENA CAVA
Vein that carries blood to the heart from the head.

AORTA
The main and longest artery in the system.

PULMONARY ARTERY
Carries blood to the lungs.

LENGTH

If you were to place all your capillaries end to end, they would be long enough to wrap twice around the world.

ARTERIES

Oxygenated blood is carried from the heart towards the cells by arteries. Arteries have elastic walls that can resist the high pressure of the blood. The capillaries that connect the arteries to the veins, carrying blood to individual cells along the way, are much thinner.

EXTERNAL TUNICA INTIMA   TUNICA MEDIA   TUNICA EXTERNA

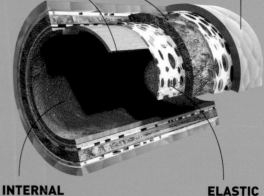

INTERNAL TUNICA INTIMA

ELASTIC LAYER

ILIAC ARTERY
Supplies blood to the pelvis and the legs.

ILIAC VEIN
The main vein in the hip.

FEMORAL ARTERY
Supplies oxygenated blood to the thigh.

INFERIOR VENA CAVA
Carries blood to the heart from the lower part of the body.

FEMORAL VEIN
Runs along the length of the thigh.

Blood

Blood is a liquid body tissue that moves through the body in blood vessels. It is made of water with substances dissolved in it, and blood cells. It carries food substances taken in through digestion to the whole body. It also carries oxygen from the lungs to body tissues and harmful carbon dioxide from the tissues back to the lungs.

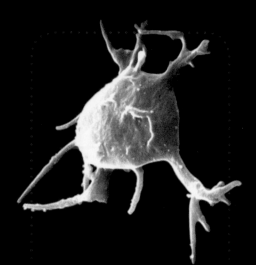

RED BLOOD CELLS
The main job of red blood cells is to absorb oxygen from the lungs and release it in other parts of the body.

WHITE BLOOD CELLS
These cells protect the body from infections by attacking bacteria, viruses and other harmful organisms.

PLATELETS
These repair broken blood vessels. They are found in wounds and help blood to clot.

RED
Red blood cells contain a protein called haemoglobin. Haemoglobin makes blood look red.

BLOOD CLOTTING

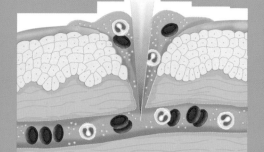

1 When the body is wounded, platelets in the blood around the wound become sticky.

2 The platelets form a cap to stop blood from exiting the wound, and release chemicals that will make the blood clot.

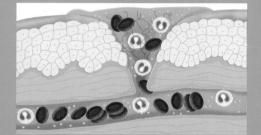

3 Cells divide to cover the damaged area.

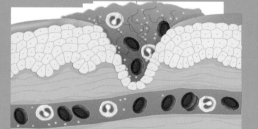

4 At the surface, a crust, or scab, forms. Underneath the crust, the damaged blood vessel repairs itself.

Respiratory system

Breathing, or respiration, is the process that allows the body to take in air. We breathe in oxygen and breathe out waste gases such as carbon dioxide. The lungs are the main organ of the respiratory system.

15

The average number of breaths per minute taken by an adult.

YAWNING

You cannot control when you yawn – it just happens. When you yawn, you take a deep breath, open your mouth very wide and stretch the muscles in the face. Yawning is a sign of tiredness, relaxation or boredom, and it is contagious – seeing someone else yawn can make you yawn yourself.

CONTINUOUS MOVEMENT

1 **Nose:** Air enters through the nostrils.

2 **Pharynx:** The air passes through the pharynx, where the tonsils detect and destroy dangerous organisms.

3 **Larynx:** The larynx is connected to the trachea. When swallowing, a flap called the epiglottis closes access to the trachea, stopping food or water from getting into the airways, and directing them instead towards the stomach.

4 **Trachea:** The trachea carries air to and from the lungs.

5 **Bronchi:** When it reaches the lungs, the trachea divides into two bronchi, one for each lung.

6 **Blood:** Oxygen passes into the blood, while carbon dioxide is passed from the blood into the air in the lungs. When you breathe out, carbon dioxide is given off.

PHARYNX
Both air and food pass through the pharynx (the upper part of the throat).

LARYNX
The vocal cords are located here.

THE RESPIRATORY PROCESS

TRACHEA
The larynx and the two bronchi are joined by the trachea.

LUNGS
There are two lungs. Here the body takes in oxygen.

BRONCHI
These branch out into bronchioles.

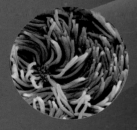

PROTECTION
The air we breathe is full of small particles that would cause us damage. The hairs in the nose and the villi in the trachea (above) trap dust and stop it from reaching the lungs.

Nervous system

There are two parts to the nervous system: the central nervous system and the peripheral nervous system. The central nervous system is made up of the brain and the spinal cord. The nerves in the rest of the body make up the peripheral nervous system.

RAPID GROWTH

The brain triples in size during the first year of life.

THE VALUE OF SLEEP

We spend a third of our lives sleeping. The brain uses this time to process information that has been gathered during the day.

100

The speed, in metres per second, at which signals can travel along the nervous system.

NERVES

Nerves look like tiny ropes made up of a large number of strands. These strands are called nerve fibres. The nerve fibres send signals from one part of the body to another.

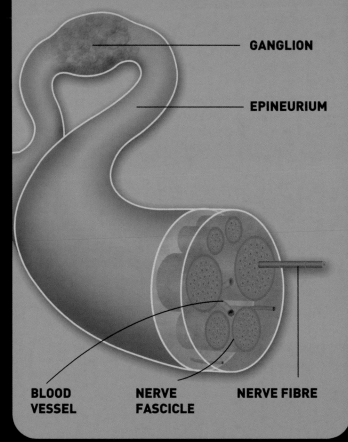

GANGLION

EPINEURIUM

BLOOD VESSEL

NERVE FASCICLE

NERVE FIBRE

REFLEXES

Reflexes are responses that you cannot control. Most reflexes are controlled by the spinal cord. The signal from the nerves is 'decoded' in the spinal cord and an instruction to react is sent out without the brain being involved.

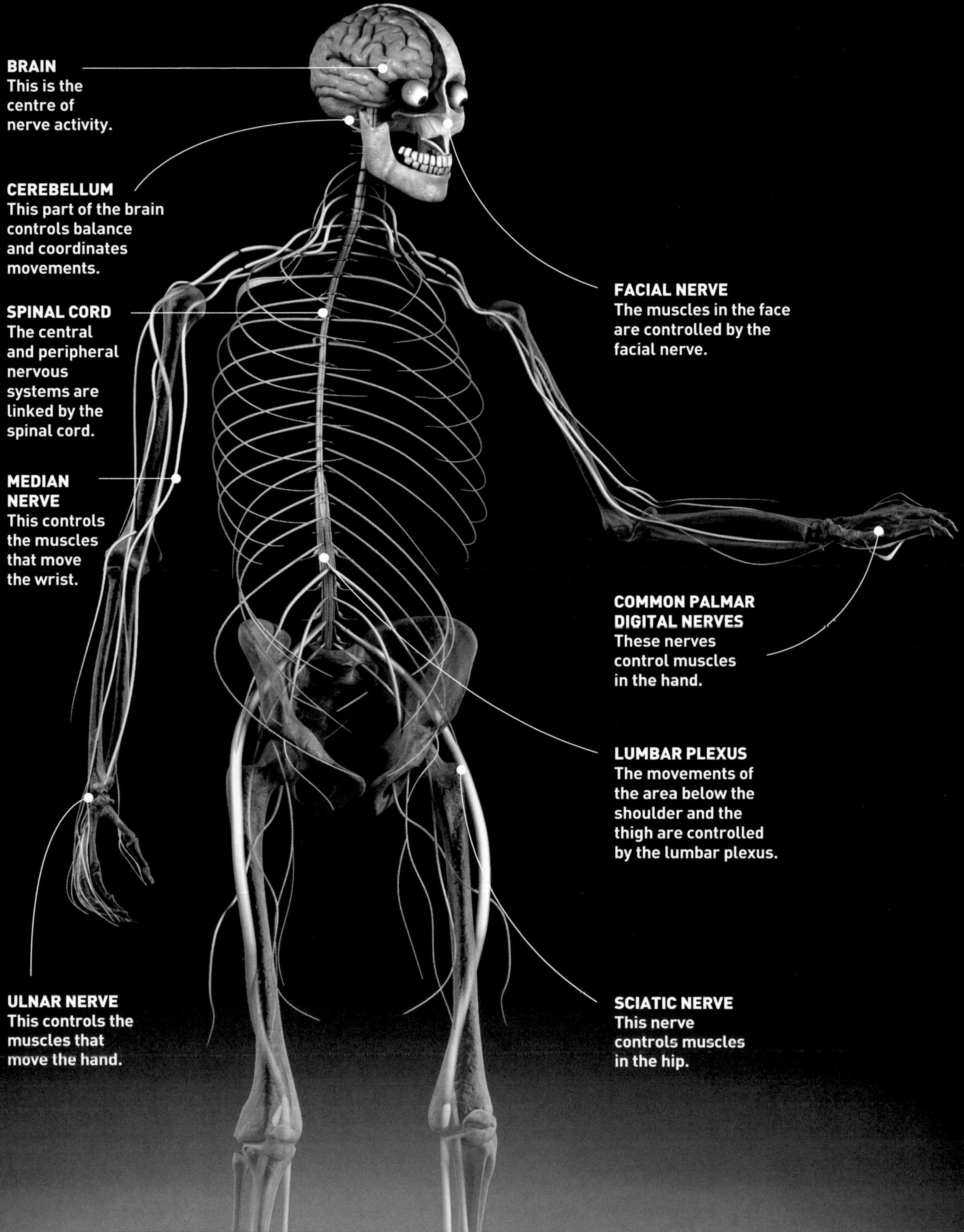

BRAIN
This is the
centre of
nerve activity.

CEREBELLUM
This part of the brain
controls balance
and coordinates
movements.

SPINAL CORD
The central
and peripheral
nervous
systems are
linked by the
spinal cord.

**MEDIAN
NERVE**
This controls
the muscles
that move
the wrist.

ULNAR NERVE
This controls the
muscles that
move the hand.

FACIAL NERVE
The muscles in the face
are controlled by the
facial nerve.

**COMMON PALMAR
DIGITAL NERVES**
These nerves
control muscles
in the hand.

LUMBAR PLEXUS
The movements of
the area below the
shoulder and the
thigh are controlled
by the lumbar plexus.

SCIATIC NERVE
This nerve
controls muscles
in the hip.

The brain

The brain is the main organ in the nervous system. It controls every action of our bodies. It is split into two hemispheres, or halves, which are in turn divided into four parts, called lobes.

1.4 KG
The weight of an adult human's brain.

TEAMWORK

There are many different areas within the brain, which must all work together. Each hemisphere is responsible for different abilities and skills. In some people, for example, the language function, usually in the left hemisphere, is swapped to the right.

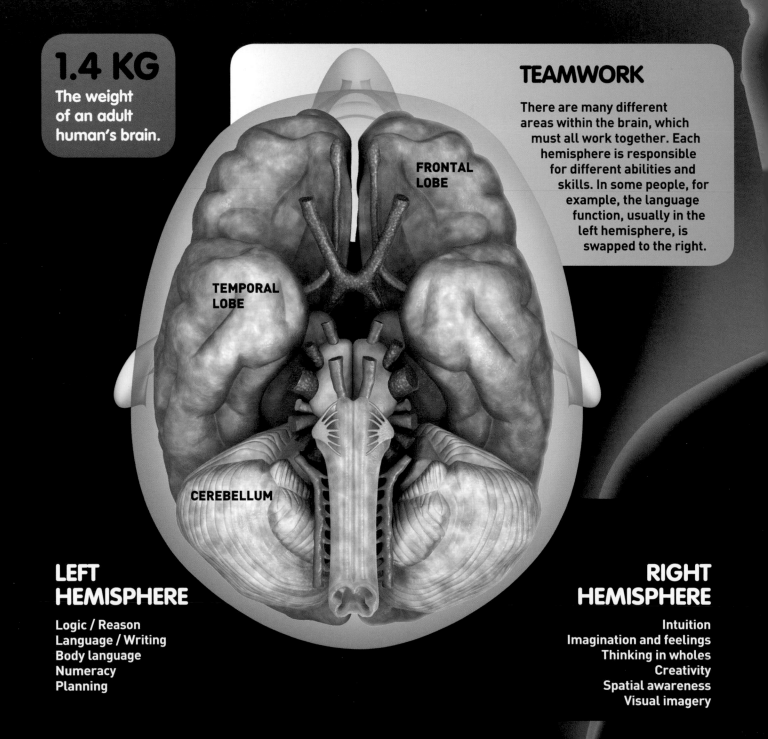

FRONTAL LOBE

TEMPORAL LOBE

CEREBELLUM

LEFT HEMISPHERE

Logic / Reason
Language / Writing
Body language
Numeracy
Planning

RIGHT HEMISPHERE

Intuition
Imagination and feelings
Thinking in wholes
Creativity
Spatial awareness
Visual imagery

THE SPINAL CORD

Located inside the backbone, the spinal cord works with the brain to form the central nervous system. Its main job is to carry nerve signals from the brain to the rest of the body. The cord is protected by the meninges, a membrane that keeps out harmful substances. Damage to the spinal cord can lead to serious disabilities, including the loss of feeling in the torso and limbs.

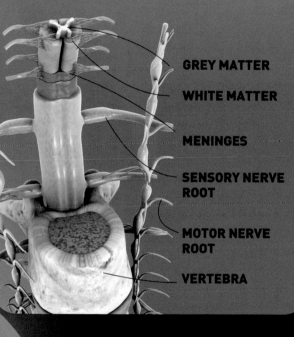

GREY MATTER

WHITE MATTER

MENINGES

SENSORY NERVE ROOT

MOTOR NERVE ROOT

VERTEBRA

OXYGEN

The human brain receives 20 per cent of the oxygen that is taken in by the lungs.

HISTORY

About 11,000 years ago, people began to settle in one place and farm the land. Soon afterwards, writing was invented and things could be written down for future generations to read. This marked the beginning of the period of recorded history. The written record tells the story of how we developed from those early days of agriculture to the modern technological world of today.

PERSIAN SOLDIER
This image of a soldier is found in the ruins of Persepolis, Iran, which was the capital city of the ancient Persian Empire (see pages 132–133).

Babylon

Of all the cities in Mesopotamia, Babylon came to be the most powerful. Babylon was founded around 2300 BC. The city is situated in modern-day Iraq. The Babylonians believed that the city belonged to the god Marduk, who appointed the king to rule in his name. The Babylonians were among the first people to use precious metals, such as gold and silver, as a form of money. They also developed new types of medicine.

FOUNDER

Babylon was founded in 2500 BC by Nimrod, a king who was believed to have built the Tower of Babel.

70 METRES

The height of the Babylonian temples, which were known as ziggurats.

THE LION OF BABYLON

This sculpture was in fact made by the Hittites, people who lived in Anatolia between the 18th and 12th centuries BC. The Lion of Babylon is now in the ruins of the palace of Nebuchadnezzar in Iraq. It is thought to have been brought there as treasure won in a war.

GODDESS OF LOVE
Ishtar was the Babylonian goddess of love, war, sex and fertility. In Sumer, she was known as Inanna.

PLANET GODDESS
The goddess Ishtar was thought to represent the planet Venus.

GOD OF WRITING
The Babylonians worshipped Nabu, the god of wisdom and writing. He was shown holding a tablet and writing tools. People believed that he used these to write down the destiny of each person.

The Indus Civilization

Like the ancient civilizations of Mesopotamia and Egypt, civilization in India developed along the banks of a river: the Indus. The river flows from the highlands down to the Arabian Sea, crossing the 3,000-kilometre-long Indian plains. The Indus Valley has large stretches of fertile land, which allowed people to settle and farm the area.

AGRICULTURE

The main crops grown in the Indus Valley were wheat, barley, root vegetables and dates.

1922

The year British archaeologists discovered one of the civilization's main cities: Mohenjo Daro.

TERRACOTTA FIGURES

In 1946, British archaeologist Sir Mortimer Wheeler discovered many small terracotta statuettes in Harappa. The statues were of women. They were thought to be goddesses of fertility. Some of them were encrusted with precious metals. As there were so many of these statues, they were probably made to be traded.

THE INDUS WRITING SYSTEM

The Indus Civilization had its own writing system, made up of at least 20 characters and more than 200 symbols. They used writing in business and also probably in places of worship. They spoke a language related to Tamil, which is still spoken in southern India.

The meaning of the symbols in the Indus writing system is not known.

PRIEST-KING

No temple buildings have been identified in the ruins of the Indus Valley. Small statues of goddesses have been found and the cities may have practised a form of religion in which the king was both a military and a spiritual leader. This sculpture is thought to be of one of these 'priest-kings'.

Fall of the Roman Empire

Many things caused the fall of the Roman Empire, including an economic crisis, power struggles, a religious crisis, and invasions from the north. Eventually, the empire could not repel the invaders. About 1,500 years ago, this vast Empire was divided into two parts.

COLONIES
The Empire was forced to leave many of its colonies, such as the one at Volubilis in North Africa, which was later occupied by Arabs.

MIDDLE AGES
The fall of the Roman Empire marked the start of the Middle Ages.

CHRISTIANITY
Christianity began to spread in the centuries after the death of Jesus. At first, Christians were treated badly because they questioned the god-status of the emperor. However, in 337 Emperor Constantine became a Christian just before he died. Soon afterwards, Christianity became the official religion of the Empire.

INVASIONS

Tribes from northern Europe – the Goths, Vandals, Franks and Huns – attacked the Roman Empire more and more often. These invasions were the reason that the last emperor was overthrown.

AD 476

The year that the Roman Empire ended in the west.

DIVISION

As the Empire stopped growing, there were no new sources of materials and slaves. It became vulnerable to economic crisis: the growing army could not be paid and the costs of administering the Empire could not be met. In time, the Empire split into two: a western empire based around Rome, and an eastern empire based around Constantinople. Emperor Theodosius (right), who died in AD 395, was the last emperor to rule both halves of the Empire.

The Renaissance and Humanism

Between the 14th and 16th centuries, Western Europe experienced an explosion in cultural and scientific achievement known as the Renaissance. A new movement, Humanism, stressed the importance of education. These movements restored the values of the ancient Greeks and Romans, breaking with the religious restrictions of the Middle Ages.

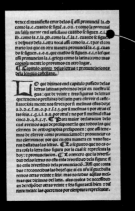

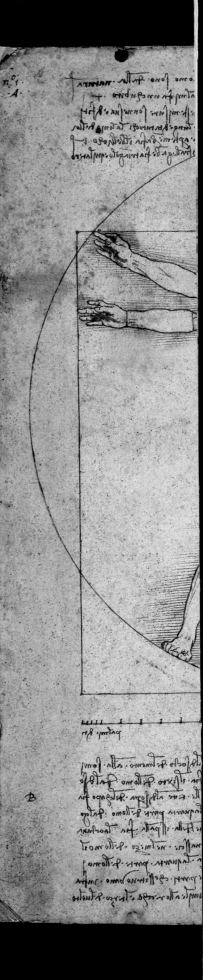

HUMANISM

Humanists stressed the importance of the individual and questioned the authority of the Church.

PRINTING PRESS
Invented by Johannes Gutenberg in around 1450, the printing press helped to spread new ideas more quickly.

MEN OF SCIENCE

During the Renaissance, scientists started to base their studies on experiments. This new way of studying science soon paid off.

LEONARDO DA VINCI
As well as being a painter, Leonardo da Vinci was also an inventor and a physicist.

NICOLAUS COPERNICUS
Copernicus suggested that the Earth revolved around the Sun. Before this, people believed that the Sun revolved around the Earth.

PARACELSUS
Paracelsus was a doctor who first studied the link between symptoms and illnesses.

A NEW VISION OF MAN

During the Middle Ages, God had been central to all art and thinking. However, the Renaissance and Humanism put humans at the centre of everything. For the first time, humans were believed to be in charge of their own destinies. This image, *Vitruvian Man* by Leonardo da Vinci, a study of the proportions of the human body, came to symbolize Renaissance thought.

FLORENCE CATHEDRAL
The Duomo, as it is commonly called, after its magnificent dome, is one of the finest churches of the Renaissance. It was designed by Filippo Brunelleschi.

ITALY, THE HEART OF THE RENAISSANCE

The Renaissance started in the prosperous city-states of Italy. Rich Italian princes used their wealth to support the new thinkers and artists.

The French Revolution

In 1789, the powerful French monarchy was overthrown, and King Louis XVI and Queen Marie Antoinette were executed, making way for a new era in which politics and justice were to be decided by the people. This was the French Revolution, which was fought under the slogan 'Liberty, Equality, Fraternity', and the Modern Age began.

JACOBINS

This group of revolutionaries were very radical and led the bloodiest years of the Revolution.

CAUSES

1. A monarchy was very rigid in a world that was changing.

2. The development of a powerful new class of people, called the bourgeoisie, who traded and became wealthy.

3. The unhappiness of the ordinary people.

4. The spread of new ideas about freedom.

5. The economic crisis that France suffered after a series of bad harvests.

THE FACES OF THE REVOLUTION

JOSEPH SIEYÈS

GEORGES JACQUES DANTON

JEAN-PAUL MARAT

THE RIGHTS OF MAN AND OF THE CITIZEN

This document was published on 26 August 1789. It laid out rights to liberty and to property, and stated that all citizens were equal before the law.

THE STORMING OF THE BASTILLE

On 14 July 1789, the people of Paris broke into the Bastille and set its prisoners free. This was an important event in the French Revolution.

A DECISIVE DECADE

The old regime was declared dead and the country was now ruled by the 'Third Estate': the bourgeoisie and the common people. This happened on 17 June 1789. The Revolution was ended by a coup that brought Napoleon Bonaparte to power in 1799.

MAXIMILIEN ROBESPIERRE

CAMILLE DESMOULIN

MARQUIS DE LAFAYETTE

LOUIS SAINT-JUST

The Industrial Revolution

Between the second half of the 18ᵗʰ century and the start of the 19ᵗʰ century, the Industrial Revolution transformed how people lived and worked. It began in Britain, then spread to the rest of Europe. Countries moved away from old ways of working and introduced factories and machines to make goods. In the 19ᵗʰ century, this process was made faster by the arrival of the railways. They could carry goods and people from place to place much more quickly and in larger numbers than ever before.

14 HOURS

The length of the working day during the Industrial Revolution.

BOOM

The European population grew rapidly during these decades, reaching 213 million in 1850.

PRODUCTION LINE

The production line was a great new way to make goods. Each worker performed just one part of the job working on specialized machines. This was a much cheaper and faster way to make goods than having each worker do the whole job.

SPINNING JENNY
A multi-spool spinning machine, the spinning Jenny was invented by Englishman James Hargreaves in 1764.

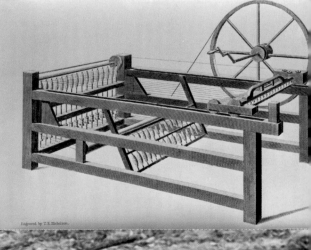

FUEL

At first, coal was the main fuel of the Industrial Age. Later, petrol became more important.

TAYLORISM

Taylor's principles were:

1. Training workers to give them specialized skills.

2. Controlling workers' time.

3. Using machines to do work where at all possible.

4. The scientific study of 'time and motion' to work out the best way to organize workers.

STEPHENSON'S ROCKET

This locomotive was powered by a new, improved steam engine. All later steam trains followed this design.

FREDERICK TAYLOR

An American engineer who came up with a system for making work more efficient.

The Russian Revolution

As World War I raged across Europe, in 1917 a revolution took place in Russia. The land and factories were taken from their owners and turned over to the peasants and workers. The Revolution was led by a communist group called the Bolsheviks, led by Vladimir Lenin. It was the first communist revolution in the world.

NICHOLAS II

The last Tsar (monarch) of Russia, Nicholas, and his family were executed by the Bolsheviks in 1918. His rule had been full of conflict, and he was a weak leader. The terrible loss of life of World War I was the final decisive factor that led to his downfall.

AGAINST THE TSAR

In February 1917, there had been demonstrations against the Tsar, which included burning tsarist symbols (below). In October, the Winter Palace, the symbol of the monarch's power, was stormed.

POWER TO THE PEOPLE

In his book *State and Revolution*, Lenin laid out his plans for a new society, in which ordinary working people – the proletariat – held political power.

SCIENCE AND CULTURE

Most places in the world have people living there. Different groups of people have developed their own ways of living, or cultures, thinking up new ideas and inventing the technology that shapes our modern lives.

CITY AT NIGHT
Today, half the world's population lives in cities such as Hong Kong (below).

Science

Throughout the ages, humans have tried to figure out how things work. Modern science uses experiments to learn more about the world and to test new ideas.

WHAT IS SCIENCE?

Scientific knowledge is based on evidence. The evidence comes from experiments that test whether or not a hypothesis is correct. If the evidence shows that a hypothesis is not correct, then scientists try to come up with a new one. A hypothesis may become a theory when there is sufficient evidence to prove it is true. It becomes the model, or theory, for the way things work.

SCIENTIFIC KNOWLEDGE

Scientists try to come up with laws to explain the way that the world works. These laws can be used to make predictions about the future. Science is:

1 **Fact-based:** Science deals with facts and events.

2 **Rational:** It is based on reason and logic, not on feelings or opinions.

3 **Verifiable:** It can be checked against data.

4 **Objective:** Scientific knowledge changes when new data is found.

5 **Systematic:** It builds on a body of knowledge, and each area of science can be tested for accuracy against this knowledge.

6 **Explanatory:** Science tries to explain how the world works.

BIOTECHNOLOGY

One of the most important branches of science is biotechnology. It uses living organisms to solve problems.

METHOD

1 Observation: Can be direct or indirect, and provides data.

2 Comparison: Tests the data you have collected against current theories and previous tests.

ADDING TO SCIENTIFIC KNOWLEDGE

According to the Austrian philosopher, Karl Popper, if you cannot test an idea in a way that might show it to be false, it does not add to scientific knowledge. This idea is called Popper's Falsification Principle.

Great scientists

Scientific discovery has been made through the hard work, intelligence and talents of many men and women. Science involves teamwork, but throughout history, brilliant individuals have come up with brand new ideas that have shaped what we know. Here are some of the most important scientists.

ALBERT EINSTEIN
(1879-1955)

Possibly the most famous scientist ever, Albert Einstein's ideas have changed the way we think of the Universe. His new ways of looking at space and time led to many new discoveries. His theories explain the force of gravity and the way that light behaves. His ideas have made many inventions possible, including the laser (which is widely used in surgery), nuclear energy and computers.

MARIE CURIE
(1867-1934)

A French-Polish mathematician, physicist and chemist, Curie worked with her husband Pierre investigating radioactivity. Curie discovered the radioactive elements radium and polonium. Her discoveries led to new treatments for cancer. Thousands of lives have been saved using treatments made possible by Curie's work. She was the first woman to receive a Nobel Prize – the top award for scientists.

DIMITRY MENDELEYEV
(1834-1907)

The Russian scientist Mendeleyev worked out how to group chemical elements. To do this, he worked out the Periodic Table, which was first published in 1869. The way he arranged the elements led to predictions that other unknown elements might exist. Years after his death, many of these elements have been found.

Archimedes
(287-212 BC)
A brilliant mechanic, Archimedes explained how levers work and invented many different machines.

Johannes Kepler
(1571-1630)
Kepler, a German astronomer, discovered laws that explained the movement of the planets around the Sun.

Robert Boyle
(1627-1691)
An Englishman who is considered the father of modern chemistry, Boyle carried out many experiments with gases. He came up with new laws to explain their behaviour.

Thomas Edison
(1847-1931)
A US physicist and inventor, Edison, developed the telegraph, a form of long-distance communication. In total, he came up with more than 1,000 inventions.

ISAAC NEWTON
(1642-1727)

An English mathematician, physicist, astronomer and philosopher, Newton contributed new ideas to many different areas of science. His theory of gravity lasted until Einstein came up with a new theory. Newton also developed a new branch of mathematics called calculus.

Max Planck
(1858-1947)
The German physicist Max Planck made the first discoveries in quantum physics. Planck discovered that subatomic particles behave in a very different way from the large things that we can see.

Ernest Rutherford
(1871-1937)
Rutherford, a physicist from New Zealand, studied the atom. He discovered that atoms all have a small nucleus at their centre surrounded by orbiting electrons.

The conquest of space

In 1957, humans sent the first artificial satellite into space. Since then, there have been many expeditions into space. Some have been manned expeditions, but most have been unmanned, sending spacecraft far out into the Solar System, or satellites to orbit the Earth. We have learned a great deal about our Universe through these voyages of discovery.

RIVALRY
The United States and Russia have been the two main countries to explore space and are great rivals.

SATELLITES
Satellites are spacecraft that orbit the Earth. They are launched into space on rockets. Many different types of satellite are now orbiting the planet. They carry out jobs such as providing telecommunications, satellite television, information about the weather and information for military uses. They send the information they gather back to Earth using radio waves.

PIONEER 10
In 1973, Pioneer 10 became the first spacecraft to orbit Jupiter. It crossed the orbit of Neptune, the outermost planet, in 1983.

SPUTNIK I
The first ever satellite was launched into space by the Soviet Union in 1957.

SPACE PROBES
Space probes are unmanned spacecraft that explore space. They are sent to study natural objects such as planets and send back information about them. They are equipped with cameras, radios to send information to Earth, and solar panels, which produce the electricity that powers them.

THE FIRST ANIMAL IN SPACE

For its second space flight, the Soviet Union launched a satellite called Sputnik II into orbit. This was the first space flight to carry a living being – a dog called Laika. The dog was connected to a machine that monitored its health. Since then, other animals, including monkeys, have been sent into space.

SPACE SHUTTLE

The space shuttle was a special kind of spacecraft that could return to Earth and fly many missions. After 135 missions, the Space Shuttle Program ended in 2011.

MANNED SPACE FLIGHT

Manned spacecraft carry equipment that provides air, water and food for the astronauts on board. They are also fitted out with areas for astronauts to relax. This equipment makes manned spaceflight very expensive. The first man in space was Yuri Gagarin, who orbited the Earth at a maximum height of 315 kilometres in 1961.

DISCOVERY

This space shuttle belongs to the United States and has completed many missions.

THOUSANDS

The number of artificial satellites that orbit the Earth.

USA

NASA Discovery

Man and the Moon

In the 'Space Race' between the Soviet Union and the United States, the Soviets put the first man in space in 1961. Eight years later, the United States put the first man on the Moon. On 20 July 1969, the Apollo 11 mission reached the Moon and two of its astronauts took the first human steps on its surface. Five more Apollo missions reached the Moon, the last one in 1972.

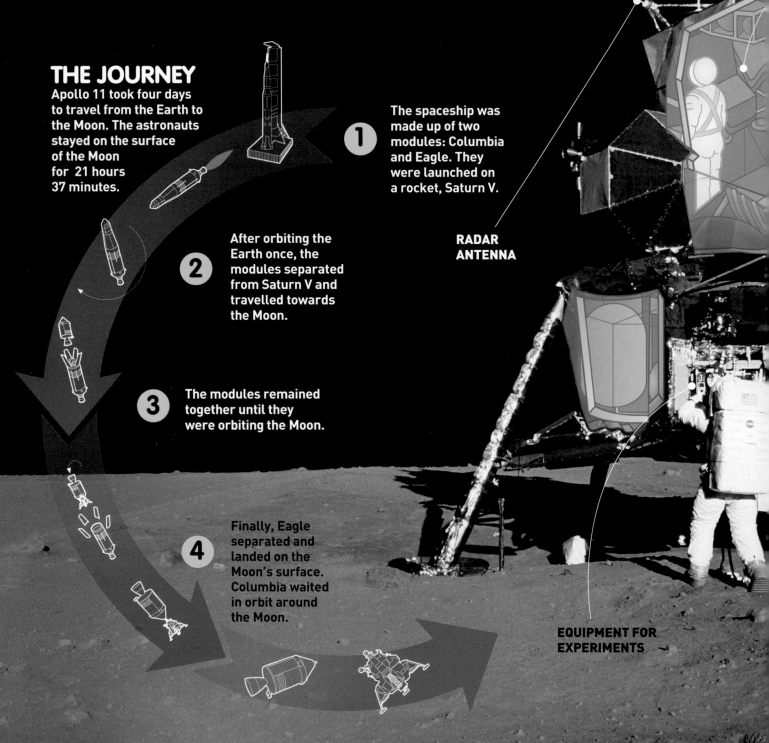

THE JOURNEY

Apollo 11 took four days to travel from the Earth to the Moon. The astronauts stayed on the surface of the Moon for 21 hours 37 minutes.

1 The spaceship was made up of two modules: Columbia and Eagle. They were launched on a rocket, Saturn V.

2 After orbiting the Earth once, the modules separated from Saturn V and travelled towards the Moon.

3 The modules remained together until they were orbiting the Moon.

4 Finally, Eagle separated and landed on the Moon's surface. Columbia waited in orbit around the Moon.

RADAR ANTENNA

EQUIPMENT FOR EXPERIMENTS

LATER MISSIONS

Apollo 11 was the first of six American missions to reach the Moon. Between 1969 and 1972, Apollos 12, 14, 15, 16 and 17 were all successful. Only Apollo 13 failed to make it, being forced to return to the Earth after an oxygen tank exploded. After six successful Moon landings, the Apollo program ended, and nobody has been back to the Moon since.

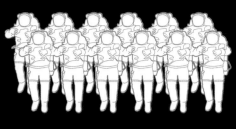

12 ASTRONAUTS HAVE WALKED ON THE MOON.

CABIN

FUEL TANK

384,400 KILOMETRES

The average distance from the Earth to the Moon.

CREW

Three highly-experienced astronauts made up the crew. All three had taken part in previous missions.

NEIL ARMSTRONG
The first human being to set foot on the Moon.

MICHAEL COLLINS
Remained in Columbia while his two colleagues landed on the Moon.

EDWIN ALDRIN
The second human being to set foot on the Moon.

SMALL STEP

As he stepped onto the Moon, Amstrong said: 'That's one small step for a man, one giant leap for mankind.'

The Internet

The Internet is a computer network that extends across the globe. To access the Internet from our homes, our computers connect with another far more powerful computer called a server. The server then sends our request along routes across the entire world. Finally, the reply arrives back at our computer. The whole process can take just a fraction of a second to complete.

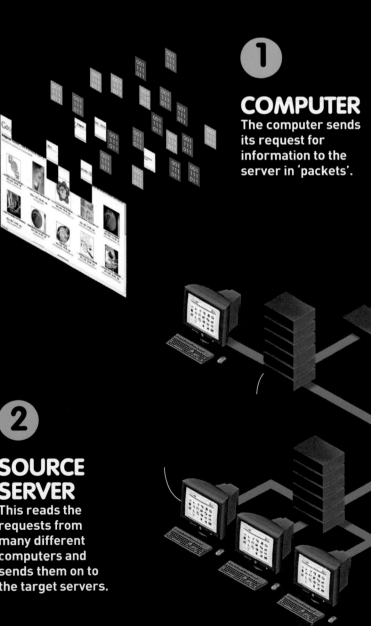

1 COMPUTER

The computer sends its request for information to the server in 'packets'.

2 SOURCE SERVER

This reads the requests from many different computers and sends them on to the target servers.

3 ROUTES

Different networks are connected to each other by routes. A router decides which is the best route to send the information along.

4

TARGET SERVER
Sends information back to
the server that requested it.

56%

**The proportion of websites
that are written in English,
the most common
language on the Internet.**

5

RECEIVING THE
INFORMATION
When the information
reaches the computer,
it is used to display the
results of the request.

2.3
BILLION

**The number of Internet users
at the beginning of 2009. The
number is constantly growing.**

ASIA
The continent with
the greatest number
of Internet users.
(45%), followed by the
United States (23%)
and Europe (22%).

Great Wall of China

The Great Wall is made up of hundreds of smaller walls that were built to defend China from invasion. It stretches thousands of kilometres across the north of the country. Walkways and corridors allowed troops to move quickly in the event of an attack.

LEGEND
The wall was called 'the stone dragon' because it resembled a dragon looking to the west.

TOWERS
Placed every 500 metres, the towers were used to keep watch. When enemy troops were spotted, smoke would be sent up from the towers.

SMOKE SIGNALS
One column of smoke from a tower signalled fewer than 500 enemies. Two columns meant a larger force. At night, fires were used instead.

WALLS
The walls are an average height of 6.5 metres, going up to 10 metres in places. The base of the walls is about 6.5 metres wide.

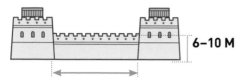

6–10 M

The distance from one tower to the next is about 500 metres.

SIGNALS
Enemy attacks were communicated from tower to tower.

FACT FILE

LOCATION China
TYPE Defensive construction
WHEN BUILT
From 221 BC to AD 1644
SIZE
6,400 kilometres long; 6–10 metres high, 6 metres wide

BUILDING
The sections built during the Ming Dynasty, which are now a tourist attraction, are made of stone and covered with bricks. Other sections are made of clay or limestone.

Wall of China

Xining • | Taiyuan • | Beijing

CHINA

BUILDING TECHNIQUES
The work was carried out during the Qin, Han and Ming dynasties. The oldest part of the wall dates from the fifth century BC. The emperor Qin Shi Huang joined up the different sections. During the Ming dynasty, it was rebuilt using a layer of mud bricks.

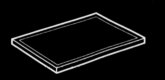

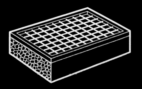

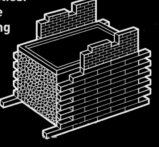

QIN DYNASTY
The first walls were made of earth and stone.

HAN DYNASTY
Wooden frames were filled with a mix of water and fine gravel.

MING DYNASTY
A mix of stone and earth was used, covered with a layer of mud bricks.

6,400 KM
The length of the wall, from the border with Korea to the Gobi Desert.

Prehistoric art

Humans have made art for thousands of years, drawing and making objects that come from their imaginations. The first drawings that we know of were made on cave walls more than 30,000 years ago. These and other early works of art often show what their makers were thinking about life and death.

ALTAMIRA
The cave of Altamira, Spain, was painted about 15,000 years ago. It is one of the finest examples of ancient cave paintings in the world.

SCULPTURES
The first sculptures were of animals that have been found on the ends of tools. Another common type of early sculpture is called a Venus figure. This takes the form of a rounded female figure, and symbolizes Mother Earth, who was believed to be the source of all life.

ARCHITECTURE
The oldest buildings are those made of huge slabs of stone. These buildings often had religious or ritual importance to the people who built them.

STONEHENGE
A circle of stones in southern England, Stonehenge is believed to have been a place for religious ceremonies, but nobody knows for sure.

CAVE PAINTINGS

Drawings of people and animals were made on the rocky sides of caves thousands of years ago.

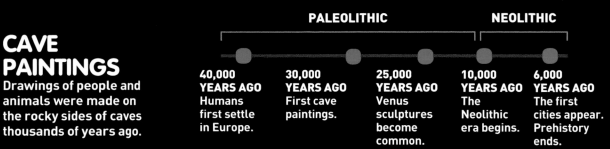

EUROPEAN PREHISTORY

PALEOLITHIC | **NEOLITHIC**

40,000 YEARS AGO
Humans first settle in Europe.

30,000 YEARS AGO
First cave paintings.

25,000 YEARS AGO
Venus sculptures become common.

10,000 YEARS AGO
The Neolithic era begins.

6,000 YEARS AGO
The first cities appear. Prehistory ends.

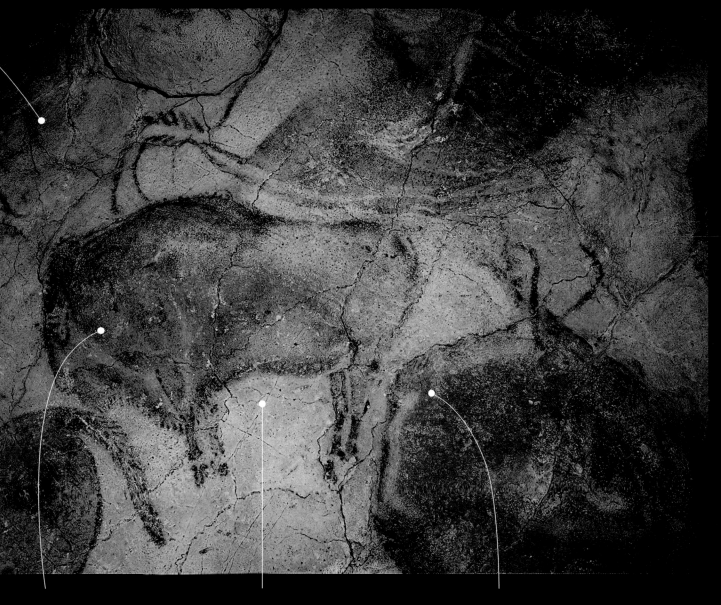

FIGURES
The most common figures in cave paintings are animals such as mammoths, bison, hyenas and horses.

REALISM
Animals are drawn very realistically. Humans appear very rarely, and are drawn in much less detail.

COLOURS
The paints were made of natural substances. Black, made from carbon, and red, made from iron oxide, were the most used colours.

GLOSSARY

ARISTOCRATIC
Describes someone who is of a high social standing, such as a nobleman.

ATMOSPHERE
The air around the Earth. The Earth's atmosphere is made up mostly of oxygen and nitrogen.

AXIS
A line through the centre of a spinning object. For example, the Earth spins on its own axis.

BACTERIA
Tiny organisms, some of which can cause disease.

BLOOD PRESSURE
A measure of the pressure at which blood flows through the body.

CALCIUM
A silvery white metal that is found in minerals such as limestone. Leaves, bones and shells all contain calcium.

CAMOUFLAGED
Something that is well-hidden. For example, the spots on a leopard help it to blend in with the tall grass so that it can sneak up on its prey.

CANAL
An artificial channel for boats and ships to sail through. In the body, a channel along which substances are passed.

CAPITALIST
Someone who supports capitalism. Capitalism is when the wealth of a country is owned by private individuals rather than by the state.

CARBON DIOXIDE
A colourless gas. Carbon dioxide is given off when humans and other animals breathe. It is also a greenhouse gas.

CELLS
The basic structural unit of all living organisms. Some animals are made up of a single cell, while others are made up of many. Cells perform all the processes to sustain life.

CIVIL RIGHTS
The rights of all of a country's citizens or people to have freedom and to be equal to each other.

COLD-BLOODED
Describes a creature that has a body temperature that changes depending on the surrounding temperature. Fish, amphibians and reptiles are cold-blooded.

COLONIZE
To control another country and make it a colony.

COMMUNIST
Someone who supports communism. Communism is a political system in which the state controls everything.

CONDENSE
To change into water, for example water vapour condenses into liquid water.

COUP
A takeover.

DEFEAT
To beat someone in a battle.

DESTINY
What is intended or meant for someone in the future.

DIET
The food a person or animal eats regularly.

DIGEST
To soften food in the stomach and intestine so that the body can absorb it.

DISSOLVED
When something has been mixed into a liquid so that it becomes part of the liquid.

DYNASTY
A series of kings or queens who come from the same family, for example, the Ming Dynasty.

EMIR
A Muslim commander or local chief.

EVAPORATION
The process of a liquid changing into a gas or vapour, for example, water evaporates to become water vapour.

EVOLUTION
The process where animals and plants develop from earlier or simpler forms of life.

FASCIST
Supporting of facism – a system of politics that is led by a dictator or person with total control or power.

FOREIGN POLICY
The way a country deals with other countries.

GALAXY
A collection of stars and dust. Our galaxy is the Milky Way.

GRAVITY
The force that pulls all objects in the Universe towards each other.

HABITAT
The natural living place of an animal or plant, for example, a lion's natural habitat is grassland or savanna.

HORMONE
A substance made in the glands of the body that is transported by the blood to stimulate organs in the body.

HUMIDITY
The amount of moisture in the air.

HYMNS
Religious songs.

HYDROGEN
A very light gas. Hydrogen has also been used to make deadly bombs.

IDEOGRAM
A character that symbolizes the idea of a thing without using the sounds used to say it. Examples are written numbers and the characters in Chinese writing.

ILLEGAL
Something that is against the law, for example, some animals are hunted illegally.

INDUSTRIALIZATION
The large-scale development of industries in a country or region.

INFINITE
Something that has no definite beginning or end.

INFLATE
To fill something with air or another gas.

LIFE CYCLE
The series of changes that an animal or plant goes through during its life.

MAGMA
A molten (melted) substance that is found beneath the Earth's crust.

MEMBRANE
A thin layer of skin, or a covering, which usually protects something else.

MILK TEETH
The first set of teeth that a human has. The milk teeth fall out and permanent adult teeth grow in their place.

MINERALS
An inorganic (non-living) substance needed by the human body for good health, such as calcium.

MOLECULES
A group of two or more atoms that are linked together in a chemical bond.

NEBULAE
Thinly spread clouds of dusts and gases.

ORBIT
To move around something, for example the Earth orbits the Sun.

ORGANISMS
A living animal or plant.

ORGANS
Parts of the body with particular functions, for example the stomach is an organ in the digestive system that helps the body to digest food.

OXYGEN
A gas found in the atmosphere that people and other animals need to stay alive. Something with oxygen is described as being oxygenated.

PREDATOR
An animal that hunts other animals. Lions and crocodiles are predators that hunt smaller animals such as antelope.

PREY
An animal that is hunted or killed by another animal, for example antelope are hunted by lions.

PROTEINS
Substances that are necessary for growth and good health. Animal proteins come from animals.

RADIATION
Heat, light or another energy source that is given out by something, for example the Sun.

REBELLION
A rise in opposition or armed resistance to an established government or leader.

REFLECT
To send something back from a surface, for example, heat, light and sound can be reflected.

REIGN
To rule a country or region, usually by a king or queen.

REPRODUCE
To make more of something, for example, humans reproduce to make children.

RITUAL
A series of actions or ceremonies, which are often religious, and take place regularly.

ROTATE
To turn around.

SHRINE
A sacred or holy place such as a temple or chapel.

SPECIES
A group of plants or animals that have the same characteristics.

SPORES
Minute, usually single-celled, reproductive units such as fungi.

TIDE
The regular rising (high tide) and falling (low tide) of the sea, which usually happens twice a day.

TOTALITARIAN
Describes a form of government that has just one political party.

TRADE
Business dealings such as the buying and selling of goods.

WARM-BLOODED
Describes a creature that has a warm body temperature that stays about the same regardless of the changes in temperature of the surroundings. Birds and mammals are warm-blooded.